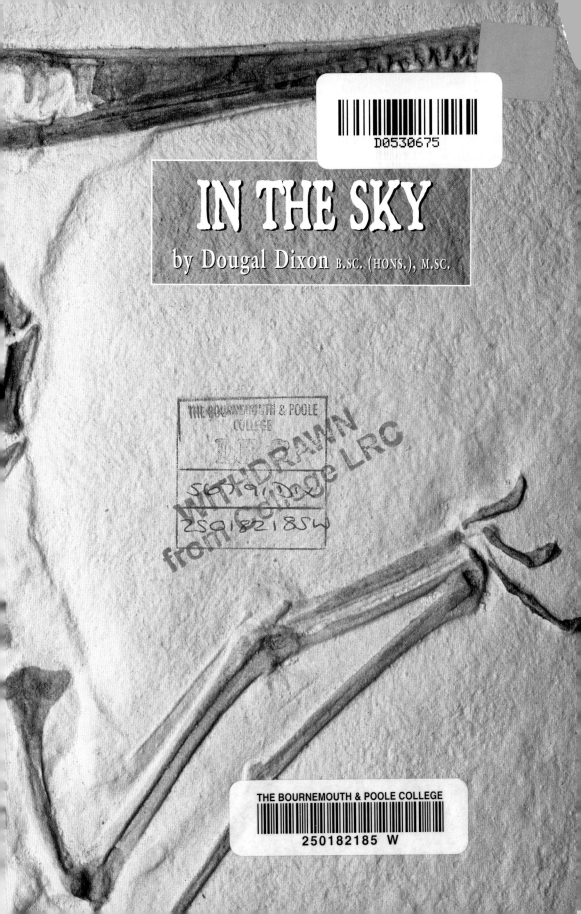

IN THE SKY

by Dougal Dixon B.SC. (HONS.), M.SC.

WING AND A PRAYER

The earliest flying reptile known was the Permian *Coelurosauravus*. It looked very much like a lizard, but its ribs were extended out to the side and supported gliding wings made of skin. The modern flying lizard of Malaysia glides in exactly the same manner.

KING OF THE SKIES

Gliders like *Coelurosauravus* were replaced in importance by the pterosaurs by late Triassic times. These famous flying reptiles were the first vertebrates to adapt to a life of active flight. They appeared at about the same time as the first dinosaurs, and became extinct at the end of the Cretaceous period. Pterosaur wings were made of reinforced skin stretched out on an arm and an elongated fourth finger.

EARLY BIRDS

Birds such as this *Sinornis* appeared about halfway through the Age of Dinosaurs, evolving from the dinosaurs themselves. Birds continue to thrive, and are the main flying vertebrates today. Their wings are made of a bony structure consisting of some of the fingers fused together, supporting feathers fanning out from the arms.

THE PIONEERS

While the dinosaurs, fish and mammals were colonizing the land and the sea in prehistoric times, the sky up above was buzzing with activity. Early flyers were simple organisms, but nature gradually came up with more complex designs. First came the insects, who continue to flourish today. Next came the flying reptiles, gliding creatures which evolved from ground-living, lizard-like animals.

These reptiles were replaced in terms of importance by the pterosaurs, probably the most famous of the ancient flying reptiles. Finally, the first birds appeared halfway through the Age of Dinosaurs, and have continued to rule the skies to this day.

AMBER PERFECTION

The best fossils come from amber preservation. When an unwary insect gets stuck in the sticky resin that oozes from tree trunks, the resin engulfs the insect and preserves it perfectly. When the tree dies and becomes buried, over a long period of time the resin solidifies and becomes the mineral we call amber. The 1994 film *Jurassic Park* was based on the premise that foreign DNA could be taken from biting insects preserved in amber to recreate the creature that was bitten. While this might not be possible today, it is an exciting concept.

THE FIRST KINGS

Meganeura was like a dragonfly, but much larger – the size of a parrot. Its wings were typical insect wings, consisting of a thin sheet of chitin, supported by a network of rigid veins. *Meganeura* lived in Carboniferous times, not long after insects first evolved.

CARBONIFEROUS/PERMIAN	TRIASSIC	EARLY/MID JURASSIC	LATE JURASSIC	EARLY/LATE CRETACEOUS
360-245 MYA	245-208 MYA	208-157 MYA	157-146 MYA	146-65 MYA

SOLAR POWERED

Kuehneosaurus was a gliding reptile
that existed in western England in late Triassic
times. It was very similar in structure to *Icarosaurus*.
There were about a dozen wing supports (about half
the number of the earlier *Coelurosauravus*),
suggesting that the wings were longer and narrower,
and probably more manoeuvrable. The skin of the
wings was probably rich in blood vessels and the
wings may have been able to warm up the
animal in the sun like a solar panel.

LONG LEGS

Late Triassic *Sharovipteryx* from central
Asia was a small lizard-like animal about the
size of a sparrow, with the most ridiculous-
looking hind legs (circled left), each one longer
than the complete length of the body.
These long legs only made sense when it
was noticed that there was the imprint of a
membrane of skin stretched between them
and the middle of the tail.

SHAROVIPTERYX IN FLIGHT

When alive, *Sharovipteryx* must have been able to glide using
the wings on its hind legs. This would not have been a very
stable type of flight, but it was probably efficient enough to
transport the reptile from one tree to another. Small skin
flaps on the forelimbs would have helped to control the flight.
With the wing membrane stretched on elongated limbs,
Sharovipteryx must have resembled a kind of a back-to-front pterosaur.
Indeed it has been suggested that it may have been among the pterosaurs' early relatives.

EARLY FLYING REPTILES

The simplest kind of flight is a gliding flight – one that needs little in the way of muscular effort. All that is required is a lightness of body, and some kind of aerofoil structure that catches the air and allows the body to be carried along upon it, like a paper dart. In modern times we see this in flying squirrels, flying lizards and even flying frogs. There were a number of flying reptiles in Permian and Triassic times, and each one evolved independently from different reptile ancestors.

LONGISQUAMA

This is a fossil of the flying reptile *Longisquama*, from late Triassic central Asia. It had a completely different type of flying mechanism. A double **SCALES** row of long scales stuck up along the backbone, each scale forming a shallow V-shape along its mid line. When spread, these would have overlapped like the feathers of a bird to give a continuous gliding surface. Perhaps they were a precursor to the evolution of feathers in birds, which appeared 60 million years later.

A FAMOUS FIND

A famous specimen of late Triassic *Icarosaurus* was discovered by a schoolboy in New Jersey, USA. The partial skeleton shows it to have been a lizard-like animal with long projections from its ribs. The angles at which the rib extensions lay suggested that the wings could have been folded back out of the way when the animal was at rest. Several decades after the discovery, the finder realized that under United States law the specimen was his by rights, and it is now lost to science, having disappeared into his private collection.

PERMIAN	TRIASSIC	EARLY/MID JURASSIC	LATE JURASSIC	EARLY/LATE CRETACEOUS
286-245 MYA	245-208 MYA	208-157 MYA	157-146 MYA	146-65 MYA

SWIMMING PTEROSAURS

In 1784, the idea was put forward that pterosaurs were not flying animals but swimming animals. This theory influenced many scientists and artists, including Johann Wagler, whose 1830 sketch (left) suggested that pterosaurs were an intermediate stage between mammals and birds.

DEVILISH PTEROSAURS

In 1840 British geologist Thomas Hawkins published a book on the fossil sea reptiles (the ichthyosaurs and plesiosaurs) that had been discovered up to that time. The frontispiece of the book was an engraving by John Martin, an English painter of biblical and historical subjects. It was a nightmare scene in which he depicted monstrous ichthyosaurs and plesiosaurs and pterosaurs that resembled bat-winged demons.

FURRY PTEROSAURS

A surprisingly modern interpretation of pterosaurs was drawn in 1843 by Edward Newman. He regarded them as flying marsupials. Although the mouse ears are inaccurate, the furry bodies and the predatory lifestyle are well in-keeping with how we now regard these creatures.

VICTORIAN TERRORS

The concrete pterosaurs (or 'pterodactyles' as they were then called) that were erected in the grounds of the Crystal Palace in south London in 1854 tell us that most Victorians still viewed these creatures as winged dragons. These were more delicate than the surrounding statues of dinosaurs and sea animals, and unfortunately most had been badly damaged or destroyed by the 1930s.

THE DISCOVERY OF THE PTEROSAURS

The first pterosaur fossil to have been scientifically studied was an almost perfect skeleton from the lithographic limestone quarries of Solnhofen in Germany, discovered in 1784 (*see pages 8/9*). Although the skeleton was just about complete, it was impossible to compare it with any animal alive at the time, so the find remained a mystery. Seventeen years later, the French pioneer naturalist Baron Georges Cuvier guessed that it was a flying animal. Since that date, scientists have come up with many different ideas of what pterosaurs were and how they existed.

JURASSIC BATS?

English geologist Sir Henry De la Beche produced a drawing in 1830 showing animal life in the Jurassic (then called Liassic) sea of southern England. It consisted of swimming reptiles, fish and ammonites, and in the air there were flying pterosaurs. De la Beche depicted pterosaurs as bat-like creatures, with their wing membranes stretching all the way down to their feet.

THE MODERN QUARRIES

The Romans excavated the fine limestone from the Solnhofen quarries to make tiles and paving stones. In the 18th century the fine-grained surface of the rock was found to be ideal for printing, and this led to the rapid expansion of the quarry workings. Despite the fact that these quarries are famous for their fossils (not only of pterosaurs, but of early birds, small dinosaurs, lizards and a whole host of marine animals), it takes the removal of a vast volume of rock to find one worthwhile skeleton.

NORTHERN EUROPE

SHALLOW WATERS
(MODERN SOUTHERN
GERMANY)

REEF

TETHYS OCEAN

SOLNHOFEN

Over millions of years the surface of the Earth has changed due to the action of plate tectonics, the name given to the activity that occurs under the Earth's surface. Hot magma rises, forcing the Earth to tear on the surface, separating previously joined landmasses. In late Jurassic times the area of southern Germany, including Solnhofen, lay in the shallows along the northern edge of the Tethys Ocean. This ocean separated Europe from Africa. Nowadays all that is left of the Tethys is the Mediterranean Sea and the drying puddles of the Black Sea, the Caspian Sea and the Aral Sea, all flanked by the mountains that were pushed up out of the Earth as the continents collided.

ANATOMY OF A LAGOON

Along the edge of the continental shelf to the north of the Tethys Ocean, a vast reef of sponges grew in the deeper waters. Remains of this reef can now be found stretching from Spain to Romania. As it approached the surface, this reef stopped growing as the sponges died and coral reefs started to grow on top of them. Eventually, a series of lagoons were formed between the reef and the land. Low islands lay across the lagoon, and these (as well as the hinterland) were arid, with only a few scraggly plants. The stagnant water in the lagoon became poisonous and killed any animal that swam or fell into it. Because fine sediment was accumulating below, these animals were preserved almost perfectly.

TRIASSIC	EARLY/MID JURASSIC	LATE JURASSIC	EARLY CRETACEOUS	LATE CRETACEOUS
245-208 MYA	208-157 MYA	157-146 MYA	146-97 MYA	97-65 MYA

SOLNHOFEN - PTEROSAUR PARADISE

Solnhofen in southern Germany has produced a treasure trove of finds – fossils so good that every detail of even the most delicate of organisms can still be seen. The rock is made of very fine particles and was formed under conditions totally lacking in oxygen, so that no further decay was possible. The technical name that geologists give to such occurrences is *lagerstatten*. There are only about a dozen such sites known, and most people regard Solnhofen as the best in the world.

THE HEADLESS ONES

Many of the pterosaur fossils found at Solnhofen are without their heads.

The probable reason is that when the pterosaurs died they fell into the shallow waters along the northern edge of the Tethys Ocean.

When the pterosaurs landed, because their bodies were so lightweight they floated at the surface for a while.

While lying on the surface, their floating bodies began to decay and their heads, being the heaviest part, fell off first.

Eventually, after their heads had fallen off, the rest of the pterosaurs' bodies sank to the lagoon floor, where they were quickly covered in fine sediment.

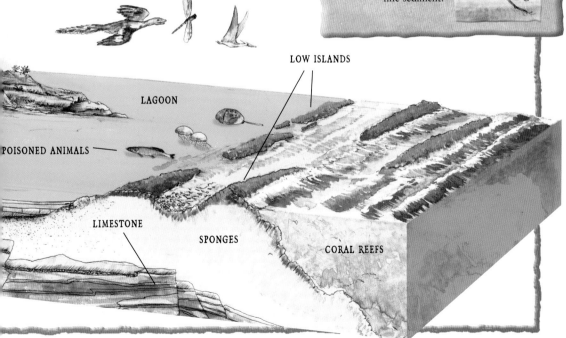

LOW ISLANDS

LAGOON

POISONED ANIMALS

LIMESTONE

SPONGES

CORAL REEFS

NARROW WINGS
PRODUCING ACTIVE,
FLAPPING FLIGHT

THE FANTASY

Many works of fiction, including the film *One Million Years BC*, show pterosaurs carrying away heavy prey like human beings in their feet or their jaws. Even if human beings had been around at that time, the pterosaurs would have been unable to do this without severely disrupting their centre of balance.

AN EDUCATED GUESS

Two good fossils of *Eudimorphodon* are known. They both have the wings folded to the body but the wing membrane has not been preserved. Nor is there any direct evidence of a furry pelt. We can, however, guess what the membrane and the fur were like by comparing the fossils with other better preserved pterosaurs (*see pages 12-13*).

LONG TAIL

TRIASSIC 245-208 MYA	EARLY/MID JURASSIC 208-157 MYA	LATE JURASSIC 157-146 MYA	EARLY CRETACEOUS 146-97 MYA	LATE CRETACEOUS 97-65 MYA

EUDIMORPHODON

Eudimorphodon had all the physical attributes of the rhamphorhynchoids. It had long, narrow wings made of skin supported by rods of gristle and a wing span of about a metre (3 ft). Because of its variety of teeth, it could eat many foods, and its furry body facilitated a constantly active lifestyle.

THE EARLIEST PTEROSAUR

The pterosaurs were the most important of the flying animals in Triassic, Jurassic and Cretaceous times. Once they evolved they quickly adopted all the features that were to remain with the group for the rest of their existence. Pterosaurs fall into two groups. The more primitive group – the rhamphorhynchoids – had long tails, short wrist bones and narrow wings. These were the the first to evolve, appearing in Triassic times. The other group – the pterodactyloids – evolved later, towards the end of the Jurassic.

SHORT
WRIST
BONES

TEETH OF
DIFFERENT
SIZES

FURRY
BODY

WING MUSCLES

The pterosaurs must have had a flying action like modern bats or birds (right). The arrangement of the shoulder bones and the wing bones show that the muscles present facilitated an active flapping flight.

CATCHING PREY

Many pterosaurs caught fish and, judging by its teeth, *Eudimorphodon* was one of them. The balance of the animal in flight was so delicate that it would not have been able to fly with a fish in its mouth. The pterosaur would have had to have swallowed the fish immediately to get it to its centre of balance.

The skeletons of *Dimorphodon* fall to pieces and are crushed easily, because they are made up of the finest struts of bone. Nevertheless there have been two good specimens found, and both of these are in the Natural History Museum in London.

JURASSIC SKIES

Above the early Jurassic shorelines the air was thick with wheeling pterosaurs. They were all of the long-tailed rhamphorhynchoid type. Within a few million years these would all have been replaced by a new pterosaur group – the short-tailed, long-necked, long-wristed pterodactyloids.

BIG HEADS

Rhamphorhynchoid pterosaurs ruled the skies during the early Jurassic period. The earliest Jurassic pterosaur known was discovered in 1828 by the famous professional collector Mary Anning. It was given the name *Dimorphodon* because of its two types of teeth. Scientists today are still in disagreement over many of its features – these disagreements are typical of our lack of knowledge of the pterosaurs in general.

BRILLIANT BEAK

Dimorphodon had two different types of teeth – good for grabbing and holding on to slippery prey such as fish. The skull was very high and narrow, and consisted of windows separated by fine struts of bone. It is very likely that the sides of the head were brightly coloured for signalling, just like the beaks of modern tall-beaked birds such as puffins or toucans.

ON THE GROUND

We know that pterosaurs like *Dimorphodon* were very adept at flight, but we are not sure of how they moved around when they were not flying. The old theory was that pterosaurs crawled like lizards, while some scientists saw them as running on their hind legs like birds, with their wings folded out of the way. However, footprints in lake sediments from South America attributed to pterosaurs show the marks of the hind feet walking in a narrow track, with marks seemingly made by the claws of the forelimbs in a wider track on each side. This suggests that pterosaurs were walking upright, using the arms like crutches or walking sticks. A final theory suggests that because of their similarity to bats, maybe they did not come to the ground at all but hung upside down from trees.

TRIASSIC 245-208 MYA	EARLY/MID JURASSIC 208-157 MYA	LATE JURASSIC 157-146 MYA	EARLY CRETACEOUS 146-97 MYA	LATE CRETACEOUS 97-65 MYA

SOFT COVERINGS

Most fossils are of sea-living animals, because sea-living animals have a better chance of falling to the sea bed and eventually becoming entombed in sedimentary rock. However, many pterosaurs lived in coastal areas or around lakes, and fell into the water when they died. Sometimes they were fossilized in environments that preserved the finest of details such as wing membranes and furry coverings.

WING STRUCTURE

The wing membrane of a pterosaur was stiffened by fine rods of gristle that fanned out from the arm and hand to the wing's trailing edge. The pattern of the gristle stiffening is the same as the arrangement of the flight feathers of a bird, and the supporting fingers of a bat's wing.

A MODERN INTERPRETATION?

It is often thought that birds are the modern equivalent of the pterosaurs. However the modern bat has more in common with the pterosaur than any bird – particularly the membranous wings and the furry covering. Pterosaurs and birds shared the Cretaceous skies, but bats did not evolve until pterosaurs died out. This in itself seems to suggest that bats rather than birds occupy the pterosaurs' niche in modern times.

THE BEST PRESERVED

This *Rhamphorhynchus* from the Solnhofen deposits in Germany is one of the best preserved pterosaur fossils we have. Even the structure of its wing membrane is visible.

TRIASSIC 245-208 MYA	EARLY/MID JURASSIC 208-157 MYA	LATE JURASSIC 157-146 MYA	EARLY CRETACEOUS 146-97 MYA	LATE CRETACEOUS 97-65 MYA

HOW WERE THE WINGS ATTACHED?

There is a great deal of uncertainty about just how the pterosaur's wings were attached to the animal. Some scientists think that the wings stretched from the arms and fourth finger to the body, and did not touch the hind limbs. Perhaps the wings were attached to the hind limbs at the knee. Alternatively, it is quite possible that the wings stretched right down to the ankle.

ATTACHED TO THE BODY   ATTACHED TO THE LEGS   ATTACHED TO THE ANKLE

FURRY PTEROSAUR

The fossil of the rhamphorhynchoid *Sordes*, discovered among late Jurassic lake deposits in Kazakhstan in 1971, proved what many palaeontologists had thought for a long time – that the pterosaurs were covered in hair. The sediment was so fine and the fossilization so complete that not only was the wing membrane preserved, but fibrous patches were visible on the whole of the body, except for the tail. The diamond-shaped flap of skin at the end of the long stiff tail was probably used for steering or for balancing during flight.

THEORY OF EVOLUTION

When the British scientist Charles Darwin visited the Galapagos islands in the 19th century, he was struck by the fact that there were a variety of different beak shapes among one family of finch. Their beak shape supported their different lifestyles – heavy beaks for cracking seeds and short beaks for pecking insects and so on. This revelation triggered Darwin's theory of evolution – the idea that over millions of years, creatures could evolve to adapt to their surroundings. The variation in shape of the heads of the various *Pterodactylus* species fits in perfectly with Darwin's theory.

PTERODACTYLUS KOCHI

PTERODACTYLUS ANTIQUANS

PTERODACTYLUS ELEGANS

DIFFERENT HEADS, DIFFERENT FOODS

There were a number of different species of *Pterodactylus*, each one adapted for a particular lifestyle and for eating a particular food. The smaller species with the tiny teeth were probably insect-eaters, while the bigger forms would probably have eaten fish or small lizards. Six species are currently acknowledged, all discovered in Solnhofen. We used to think that there were far more, but many of these finds have subsequently turned out to be juveniles of known species.

TRIASSIC 245-208 MYA	EARLY/MID JURASSIC 208-157 MYA	LATE JURASSIC 157-146 MYA	EARLY CRETACEOUS 146-97 MYA	LATE CRETACEOUS 97-65 MYA

THE MOST FAMOUS

It is *Pterodactylus* that gives the pterodactyloid group its name, and indeed pterosaurs are commonly referred to as 'pterodactyls'. The pterodactyloids dominated in late Jurassic times, but there have been several different types found dating from this time, so their evolution must have been under way somewhat earlier.

PTERODACTYLUS FOSSIL

As with *Rhamphorhynchus*, the best specimens of *Pterodactylus* have been found in the limestone deposits of Solnhofen. They clearly show the details of the skeleton and occasionally the imprints of the wing membranes. Sometimes there is even the imprint of a throat pouch rather like that of a pelican. Other remains of *Pterodactylus* have been found in similar-aged rocks on the south coast of England and in the dinosaur-rich deposits of Tanzania in Africa.

PTERODACTYLUS IN FLIGHT

There is little doubt that the pterodactyloids originally evolved from the rhamphorhynchoids, but *Pterodactylus* does have several differences from the group. Its head and neck are longer than in the rhamphorhynchoids, and the neck vertebrae are particularly long. The head meets the neck at a right angle, rather than being in a straight line, and its skull more lightly-built. *Pterodactylus* has a short tail, with no steering or flying function, and its long wrist bones mean that the three fingers of the 'hand' are farther down the wing.

A QUESTION OF CRESTS

Many pterosaurs had spectacular crests that allowed them to signal to one another and to enable them to identify members of their own species.

Pteranodon, with its backward-pointing crest, is the most famous of the crested pterosaurs. Its crest may have been used to help it with steering through the sky.

PTERANODON

Tropeognathus had semicircular crests on its upper and lower jaws. This crest arrangement may have helped to cleave the water as the pterosaur dipped into the waves for fish while still on the wing.

TROPEOGNATHUS

TAPEJARA

Tapejara was characterized by a tall, bony crest at the front of its skull, probably supporting a flap of skin behind.

TUPUXUARA

Tupuxuara had a crest that consisted of a vast plate of bone reaching up and beyond the back of the skull. It was full of blood vessels and so it must have been covered in skin. Perhaps it had a heat-regulating function as well as being used for display.

HEADS & CRESTS

There are birds of every kind today, ranging from perching birds and swimming birds to wading birds and hunting birds. Modern birds have a variety of different heads and beaks – deep, strong beaks for cracking nuts; long, pointed beaks for probing mud; short, sharp beaks for pecking insects; and hooked beaks for tearing flesh.

This variety was just as pronounced among the pterodactyloids. As the Age of Reptiles continued, they diversified into all different types, and had different head shapes to suit their different lifestyles.

HIDEOUS FIND

One of the most grotesque of the pterosaurs was *Dsungaripterus*. It had a beak like a pair of upturned forceps, a battery of crushing, tooth-like, bony knobs at the back of the jaws and a crest that stretched from the back of the head to the snout. It was a large pterosaur with a wingspan of over three metres (10 ft). *Dsungaripterus* was the first pterosaur to have been discovered in China.

DSUNGARIPTERUS RESTORED

We can usually tell how an animal lived and what it ate by looking at its jaws. *Dsungaripterus*, from the early Cretaceous period, probably ate shellfish. The narrow pointed jaws could have been used for winkling out shellfish from rocky crannies, and the shells would have been crushed by the tooth-like knobs in the back of their jaws. The crest would have been brightly coloured and was probably used for signalling to other pterosaurs.

TRIASSIC	EARLY/MID JURASSIC	LATE JURASSIC	EARLY CRETACEOUS	LATE CRETACEOUS
245-208 MYA	208-157 MYA	157-146 MYA	146-97 MYA	97-65 MYA

PTERANODON SKELETON

This partial skeleton of the giant pterosaur *Pteranodon* was found in Cretaceous rocks in Kansas, USA. It shows a skull fragment, the bones of the wing finger and the complete hind legs. The whole skeleton was extremely lightweight, and the bones had openings to allow the penetration of air sacks, connected to the lungs. This system is seen in modern birds.

QUETZALCOATLUS

PTERANODON

ARGENTAVIS

A FLIGHT OF MONSTERS

Pteranodon has the perception of being the largest of the pterosaurs. The biggest species of *Pteranodon* had a wingspan of about 9 metres (30 ft). However, in the 1970s remains from an even larger pterosaur were found in late Cretaceous rocks in Texas. It was given the name *Quetzalcoatlus*, after the flying serpent from Aztec mythology. All sorts of different estimates were made about the size of this beast. The current estimate is that it had a wingspan of about 11–12 metres (36–39 ft). The biggest bird known is the condor-like *Argentavis* from Argentina, which existed around 35 million years ago. It had a wingspan of 7 metres (25 ft). Among living birds, the royal albatross has the biggest wingspan, reaching 3 metres (10 ft).

THE BIGGEST

Pteranodon was discovered in the 1870s in the late Cretaceous beds of Kansas in the United States. It had a wingspan of over 9 metres (30 ft). Science was astounded, since this was before the development of powered aviation and nobody had really experimented with the sizes of flying structures. Now it looks pretty modest when compared with some more recent discoveries.

THE BIGGEST - FOR THE MOMENT

The current record holder is *Arambourgiania*, a pterodactyloid that may have had a wingspan of about 12 metres (39 ft). It had an extremely long neck, and when the neck bones were first found they were thought to have been the long finger bones that supported the wing. The original name given to it was *Titanopteryx*, but that name had already been given to something else, so the title had to be changed.

THE SMALLEST - FOR THE MOMENT

At the other end of the scale, the tiny pterosaur *Anurognathus* holds the record for the smallest pterosaur known. It had a wingspan of about 50 cm (2 ft). Its short head contained little peg-like teeth, ideal for catching and crushing insects. Despite its short pterodactyloid-like tail, it is actually a member of the more primitive rhamphorhynchoids. Only one skeleton has been found, and that was in the late Jurassic Solnhofen deposits (*see page 8/9*).

TRIASSIC	EARLY/MID JURASSIC	LATE JURASSIC	EARLY CRETACEOUS	LATE CRETACEOUS
245-208 MYA	208-157 MYA	157-146 MYA	146-97 MYA	97-65 MYA

THE FIRST BIRD

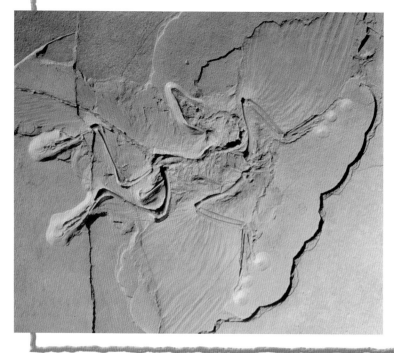

FEATHER

The first *Archaeopteryx* fossil to be found was just the feather. In isolation it looks like nothing unusual. It is a perfectly conventional flight feather as could be found on a modern bird. The main support is a vane that is off-centre, showing that it is from a wing and used for flight. The filaments forming the vane of the feather had rows of hooks that enabled them to fix to one another to give stability – just as in a modern bird. There was a downy portion at the base for insulation, as modern birds have. It was discovered just a year before the first partial skeleton was found.

I n 1859 Charles Darwin published *The Origin of Species*, creating an immediate row. How could animals have evolved into different types over a long period if they had all been created at the same time, as it says in the Bible? The scientific community found itself in opposition to the overpowering influence of traditional biblical teaching. Then, two years later, a remarkable fossil was discovered in the quarries of Solnhofen (*see page 8/9*). It was obviously a dinosaur, but it sported bird's wings and was covered in feathers. Here were the remains of a creature that appeared to be a stage in the evolution of birds from dinosaurs. Today, few scientists dispute the notion that *Archaeopteryx* (as this creature was named) evolved from dinosaur ancestors.

VINDICATING DARWIN

Eight *Archaeopteryx* fossils have been found so far, all from the Solnhofen quarries, ranging in quality from a single feather to an almost complete bony skeleton with feathers. One was found in a private collection, having been misidentified as the small dinosaur *Compsognathus*. This specimen did not show the feathers, and the misidentification serves to emphasize the resemblance between the primitive bird and the dinosaur ancestor.

THE LIVING ARCHAEOPTERYX

Had we seen *Archaeopteryx* in life, fluttering away from us, there would be no doubt in our minds that we were looking at a bird, albeit a rather clumsy one. However, a closer look would reveal a set of toothed jaws, just like a dinosaur, instead of the usual bird beak. The tail appeared to be paddle-shaped, unlike a modern bird's muscular stump with a bunch of feathers. This tail was a stiff straight rod, like a dinosaur's tail, with feathers growing from each side. The final oddity would be the claws, three of them protruding from the leading edge of the wing. All in all, *Archaeopteryx* would have appeared part bird, part dinosaur.

COVERTS   PRIMARIES

CLAWS   SECONDARIES

THE WING

The wing of *Archaeopteryx* was no halfway measure. Apart from the clawed fingers it was identical in structure to the wing of a modern flying bird, with the elongated finger-like primary feathers, bunched secondaries and coverts streamlining the whole structure. The wing muscles would have been weaker than those of a modern bird as there was no strong keeled breastbone to anchor them, but the flying action must have been the same.

TRIASSIC	EARLY/MID JURASSIC	LATE JURASSIC	EARLY CRETACEOUS	LATE CRETACEOUS
245-208 MYA	208-157 MYA	157-146 MYA	146-97 MYA	97-65 MYA

CAUDIPTERYX'S ENVIRONMENT

Caudipteryx (foreground), part of the Chinese 'Gang of Three', lived in an environment like the one shown above.
Forests of conifers and ginkgoes, with an undergrowth of ferns and cycads, provided refuge and food for all sorts
of different animals in late Jurassic and early Cretaceous China. Lizards and small mammals scampered through the
undergrowth and little feathered theropod dinosaurs hunted between the trees. The air was colonized by birds
(some looking rather like modern types), while on the ground raced several different half-dinosaur, half-bird creatures.

UTAHRAPTOR

DEINONYCHUS

VELOCIRAPTOR

BAMBIRAPTOR

MANIRAPTORAN DINOSAURS

The group of meat-eating
dinosaurs known as the
maniraptorans have always been
recognized as being very bird-like
animals. Attempts have been
made to put them on the
ancestral tree of the birds,
but the problem is that, being
late Cretaceous dinosaurs, they
were much later than the first
bird *Archaeopteryx*. Perhaps the
maniraptorans evolved from
Archaeopteryx, or *Archaeopteryx*-
like birds that lost their powers of
flight. If that were the case, they
would have been very much like
the Chinese 'Gang of Three'.

CHINESE 'GANG OF THREE'

Across the contemporary European-Asian landmass, where China's Liaoning province now lies, a series of forest-shrouded inland lakes produced fossils that were just as spectactular as those from Solnhofen. These include three kinds of animal that, like *Archaeopteryx*, show the evolutionary connection between birds and dinosaurs. Only recently, with improved scientific exchanges between China and the West, is their true significance being fully appreciated.

SINOSAURIPTERYX

One of the little dinosaurs present in the Liaoning province was *Sinosauropteryx*. It seems to have been covered in fur or feathers. The preservation is so good that a kind of downy fuzz is visible all around the bones. Although there is still some dissent, most scientists are convinced that this represents a covering of 'protofeathers', structures that are part way between hair, like that of a mammal, and feathers, like those of a bird.

SINOSAUROPTERYX FOSSIL

Only the downy covering on this skeleton shows *Sinosauropteryx* to have been related to the birds. Apart from that, it is pure meat-eating dinosaur. The long legs and tail show it to have been a swift-running animal, while the short arms were armed with three claws. Three skeletons of *Sinosauropteryx* have been found, and their stomach contents show that they hunted lizards and small mammals that existed at that time.

HALF-BIRD, HALF-DINOSAUR

Another small animal was *Protarchaeoteryx*. It was about the same size as *Sinosauropteryx* but it had a short tail and much longer arms. It was also covered in fuzz and, although the only skeleton found was very jumbled up, there seemed to be long feathers along the arms and tail. The feathers on the arms would have given a wing-like structure, but it would not have been sufficent to give the animal any power of flight.

TRIASSIC	EARLY/MID JURASSIC	LATE JURASSIC	EARLY CRETACEOUS	LATE CRETACEOUS
245-208 MYA	208-157 MYA	157-146 MYA	146-97 MYA	97-65 MYA

THE FIRST BEAK

Confuciusornis is the first beaked bird that we know of. A beak is a much more practical, lightweight alternative to the heavy teeth and jaws of a reptile. It consists of a sliver of bone, sheathed in a lightweight horny substance that combines strength with lightness. Anything that reduces their weight is an advantage to a flying animal.

ALULA

FLIGHT CONTROL

Eoalulavis from early Cretaceous lake deposits in Spain is the first bird that we know to have carried an alula. This is a tuft of feathers on the leading edge of the wing, more-or-less where our thumb is. With very small movements of this structure the passage of air over the wing can be altered considerably, and this makes the flight much more controllable. All modern birds have this. However, fossils of *Eoalulavis* are unclear about whether or not the bird had other advanced features such as a beak or a pygostyle.

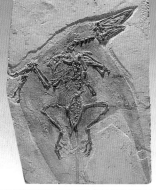

CONFUCIUSORNIS FOSSIL

Many hundreds of fossils of *Confuciusornis* have been uncovered at the Liaoning site in China. Some are so well preserved that the details of the plumage are clear. Some have long tail feathers, like those of a bird of paradise, while others have none. This suggests that, as in modern birds, the males had much more flamboyant plumage than the females.

TOWARDS MODERN BIRDS

For all its fine feathers, *Archaeopteryx* was still mostly dinosaur. It had a long reptilian tail, fingers on the wings and a jaw full of teeth. Modern birds have stumpy tails called pygostyles, supporting long feathers. Their wing fingers have completely disappeared, and they also have beaks instead of jaws and teeth. These are all weight-saving adaptations, evolved to make the bird as light as possible so that it can fly more efficiently. These features seem to have appeared at different times during the Age of Dinosaurs.

A MODERN TAIL

Iberomesornis, a fossil bird from early Cretaceous rocks in Spain, is the earliest bird known to have a pygostyle tail. This structure consists of a muscular stump from which the tail feathers grow in a fan arrangement. The muscles of the pygostyle can spread the tail feathers out or bunch them together, helping to control flight or make a display for courting purposes.

THE PERCHING FOOT

Birds that live in trees usually have feet in which the first toe is turned backwards, enabling the foot to grasp a small branch so the bird can perch. An early example of a perching foot is found in *Changchengornis* – a close relative of *Confuciusornis* – also found in the Liaoning rocks in China. This bird also had a hooked beak, suggesting that it was a meat-eater like a hawk.

Hesperornis was a swimming bird of late Cretaceous North America. As big as a man, it must have looked something like a penguin, but with no forelimbs at all, and a long beak full of teeth. This leg bone was found in the chalk deposits in West Kansas, United States.

THE DINOSAUR RE-EVOLVED?

Once the dinosaurs died out, a number of huge, flightless hunting birds evolved around 65 million years ago. *Phorusrhachos* of South America and *Diatryma* of North America were built along the lines of medium-sized meat-eating dinosaurs, with fast hind legs and fierce heads. *Titanis* (above) from Florida even had tiny clawed hands on the remains of its wings. It is almost as if there had still been a niche for dinosaur-shaped hunting creatures and evolution had filled it with giant hunting birds.

KILLER DUCK

Bullockornis lived in Australia around 20 million years ago. It stood 3 metres (10 ft) high and had a huge beak that was either used for cracking nuts or tearing flesh. An enlarged brain capacity suggests that the latter was more likely, as quick senses are necessary for hunting down prey. It was unrelated to the emus or the cassowaries, or any other type of flightless bird that exists in Australia today. Despite its dinosaur-like appearance, *Bullockornis* was actually a kind of a duck.

ABANDONING FLIGHT

It is a fact that no sooner has a feature evolved than there are certain lines of evolution that abandon it. As soon as flight evolved, some birds reverted to living on the ground. There are several explanations for this. Perhaps flightless birds evolved in areas where there were no dangerous predators on the ground and so there was no need to fly, or perhaps food was more plentiful on the ground.

DEAD AS A DODO

Probably the best known of the extinct flightless birds is *Raphus*, the dodo. It evolved from pigeon stock into a ground-dwelling plant-eater on the island of Mauritius. It survived there happily for thousands of years, as there were no ground-living predators. Everything changed, however, when humans arrived on the island, and the bird was wiped out within a few years.

PLANT-EATERS

Not only were the shapes of the meat-eating dinosaurs reflected in some of the later birds, but there seemed to be bird versions of the long-necked plant-eaters as well. *Dinorinis*, the moa, existed in New Zealand right up until modern times. It thrived there because there were no ground-living predators in New Zealand – until human beings came along and caused its extinction.

LATE CRETACEOUS 97-65 MYA	PALEOGENE 65-23 MYA	NEOGENE 23-1.8 MYA	QUATERNARY 1.8-0.01 MYA

29

SINCE THE DINOSAURS

The end of the Cretaceous period was marked by a mass extinction. However, the birds lost only three quarters of their species and the remainder soon re-established themselves as the masters of the skies. As the mammals spread in the absence of dinosaurs, so they took to the skies as well. The bats developed as a successful group, and other mammal groups developed gliding forms. There were even gliding reptiles and amphibians. Throughout all this, the insects continued to buzz, as they have done since Carboniferous times.

THE WEBBED WAY

The birds that survived the mass extinction went on to become the true masters of the skies. The birds of today mostly fly, but they can also perch, wade, swim and even burrow. *Presbyornis* was a long-legged wading duck that lived in huge flocks in North America around 65 million years ago. Although it had webbed feet, its legs would have been too long to allow it to swim. The webs probably developed to prevent it from sinking into the mud.

THE TRUE KINGS

Insects appeared nearly 400 million years ago, and immediately evolved flying types. Few died out in the end-Cretaceous mass extinction, and they are now far more diverse than any other group of creatures. Wings are the tough parts of an insect's anatomy, and it is mostly wings that have been fossilized. Occasionally the preservation is so good that the patterns and markings are preserved, although the colours have long since changed.

LATE CRETACEOUS 97-65 MYA	PALEOGENE 65-23 MYA	NEOGENE 23-1.8 MYA	QUATERNARY 1.8-0.01 MYA

MODERN GLIDERS

In modern forests, there are gliding squirrels (right) that float from tree to tree by means of flaps of skin (patagia) between their limbs. This is not a new development. In lake deposits in Germany, a splendidly preserved fossil of a gliding mammal around 23 million years old has been found. Only 10 cm (4 inches) long, *Eomys* shows the presence of patagia between the limbs. It was a kind of a rodent, like modern squirrels.

AN EARLY BAT

In the early Tertiary period, not long after the extinction of the pterosaurs, the bats appeared. *Icaronycteris* would have been almost indistinguishable from modern bats. The only differences were the primitive teeth, the claw on the thumb and the first finger (modern bats only have a claw on the thumb), and the long tail that was not connected to the hind legs by the web of skin. In modern bats, the tail is completely joined to the wing membrane.

DID YOU KNOW?

There are two kinds of flight in the animal kingdom – flapping flight and gliding flight. In the first the animal must provide all the muscular energy to produce the flying action. The second relies simply upon the ability of a certain shape of wing to plane through the air.

Flapping flight is seen in birds and in pterosaurs. Occasionally this may lapse into the first or second kinds of gliding flight, as when a vulture soars on rising hot air looking for food, or an albatross skims the wave surfaces of the ocean. Watch a pigeon displaying – it flaps its way up to a particular height and then glides downwards as if on a roller coaster, and then flaps upwards again. Presumably the pterosaurs of old had habits like this too, using a variety of flying techniques.

Two types of gliding flight are recognized. In the first the gliding action is initiated by the animal's own muscular efforts. This is seen in flying fish, which launch themselves into the air by a fast swim in a slanting trajectory to the surface. Such flight only lasts a few seconds. In the second the animal simply drops into the air from a high vantage point and relies on its aerodynamic shape to take it to where it wants to go – like a hang-glider down a slope of air. Flying squirrels, flying frogs and the flying dragon lizard of Malaysia use this kind of gliding, taking them from a high perch on one tree to a lower level on another.

Scientists disagree as to how bird flight evolved. Some say that the primitive birds, like *Archaeopteryx*, started as gliders, planing down from high tree branches. Others see them as essentially terrestrial creatures launching themselves into the air by running quickly along the ground.

ACKNOWLEDGEMENTS

We would like to thank: Advocate and Elizabeth Wiggans for their assistance.
Illustrations by John Alston, Lisa Alderson, Simon Mendez and Luis Rey.
Copyright © 2004 *ticktock* Entertainment Ltd.
First published in Great Britain by ticktock Publishing Ltd., Unit 2, Orchard Business Centre, North Farm Road, Tunbridge Wells, Kent TN2 3XF.
All rights reserved.
No part of this publication may be reproduced, stored in a retrieval system, or transmitted in any form or by any means electronic, mechanical, photocopying, recording or otherwise, without prior written permission of the copyright owner.
A CIP catalogue record for this book is available from the British Library. ISBN 1 86007 235 6 (paperback). ISBN 1 86007 239 9 (hardback).

Picture Credits:
t=top, b=bottom, c=centre, l=left, r=right, OFC=outside front cover, IFC=inside front cover, IBC=inside back cover, OBC=outside back cover

Lisa Alderson: 4b, 13b, 14-15c, 20l, 24b, 25t, 29bl. John Alston: 8cl, 9b, 9tr, 11c, 11bl, 11br, 15t. BBC Natural History Unit: 14cl.
Corbis: 8t, 14b, 16cr. Dr Peter Griffiths: 22t, 22b, 23cr. Simon Mendez: 2-3, 4-5c, 12c, 13t, 16c, 18t, 25t, 26t, 27t, 27b, 28c, 30cl.
Natural History Museum: 3t, 6t, 10b, 12t, 16t, 21cr, 29t. National Museum of Wales: 7c, 18b. Paleontologisk museum, Oslo: 4cl, 5cr, 26b.
Luis Rey: 5b, 10cl, 17c, 19c, 20-21c, 23c, 24t, 25bl, 28cl, 30-31c.

Every effort has been made to trace the copyright holders and we apologize in advance for any unintentional omissions.
We would be pleased to insert the appropriate acknowledgement in any subsequent edition of this publication.

snapping-turtle
guide